The Relations And Development Of The Mind And Brain

Elmer Gates

In the interest of creating a more extensive selection of rare historical book reprints, we have chosen to reproduce this title even though it may possibly have occasional imperfections such as missing and blurred pages, missing text, poor pictures, markings, dark backgrounds and other reproduction issues beyond our control. Because this work is culturally important, we have made it available as a part of our commitment to protecting, preserving and promoting the world's literature. Thank you for your understanding.

THE

Relations and Development

OF THE

Mind and Brain

BY

PROFESSOR ELMER GATES

~~Smithsonian Institute, Washington, D. C.~~
Director of the Laboratory of Psychology and Psychurgy, Chevy Chase, Md.

NEW YORK.
THEOSOPHICAL SOCIETY,
PUBLISHING DEPARTMENT,
244 LENOX AVE.
1904.

Copyright, 1908,
The Philosophic Company.

Copyright, 1904.
THEOSOPHICAL SOCIETY,
Publishing Department.

CONTENTS

PUBLISHER'S PREFACE.

I. THE ART OF MIND BUILDING.

II. OLD AND NEW PHRENOLOGY.
(A LETTER.)

III. PSYCHOLOGY AND PSYCHURGY.

PUBLISHER'S PREFACE.

Since the articles which comprise this little book were published in THE METAPHYSICAL MAGAZINE, there has been a constant demand for a handy form of them for convenient reference and use. The subject as presented by Professor Gates, appeals to thousands who do not have time or opportunity to enter into extensive studies in psychology, and the results of his discoveries prove intensely interesting to all active minds regardless of previous experience. They represent original work of great importance at the present time. The continuous demand being made, is our reason for reproducing the writings in this form which, we trust, will meet the requirements.

We believe that further investigations in similar lines to those described by Professor Gates will help to solve some, at least, of the mysteries of the mind.

The Art of Mind Building

I
THE ART OF MIND-BUILDING.*

The first experiment in my investigations regarding the mind consisted in giving certain animals an extraordinary and excessive training in one mental faculty—e.g., seeing or hearing—and in depriving other animals, identical in age and breed, of the opportunity of using that faculty. I then killed both classes of animals and examined their brains to see if any structural difference had been caused by excessive mental activity, as compared with the deprivation or absence thereof. During five or six months, for five or six hours each day, I trained dogs in discriminating colors. The result was that upon examining the occipital areas of their brains I found a far greater number of brain-cells than any animal of like breed ever possessed.

These experiments serve to localize mental functions, and, above all, to demonstrate the fact that more brains can be given to an animal, or a human being, in consequence of a better use of the mental faculties. The trained dogs were able to discriminate between seven shades of red and six

---
* A personal interview, especially reported for the THE METAPHYSICAL MAGVZINE, by George J. Manson.

or eight of green, besides manifesting in other ways more mental ability than any untrained dog.

"The application of these principals to human education is obvious. A child that has been trained for six weeks after birth in the excessive use of the temperature senses (detection of heat and cold) was found, after dying of scarlet fever, to possess in the temperature areas of the brain more than twenty-four times the average number of cells. As a matter of fact, the child was able to detect differences in temperature unrecognizable by other children of its age.

Under usual circumstances and education, children develop less than ten per cent. of the cells in their brain areas.. By processes of brain-building, however, more cells can be put in these otherwise fallow areas, the child thus acquiring a better brain and more power of mind. Brain-building should properly begin a few weeks after birth, because, as soon as the brain is fully developed in all its areas, the child is prepared to acquire, by technical and professional education, special knowledge and particular kinds of skill. If the child has manifested artistic ability, this course of brain-building will not only increase that talent but provide supplementary development to prevent one-sidedness and disease.

In 1879 I published a report of experiments showing that, when the breath of a patient was passed through a tube cooled with ice so as to condense the volatile qualities of the respiration, the iodide of rhodopsin, mingled with these condensed products, produced no observable precipitate. But, within five minutes after the patient became angry, there appeared a brownish precipitate, which indicates the presence of a chemical compound produced by the emotion. This compound, extracted and administered to men and animals, caused stimulation and excitement. Extreme sorrow, such as mourning for the loss of a child recently deceased, produced a gray precipitate; remorse, a pink precipitate, etc. My experiments show that irascible, malevolent, and depressing emotions generate in the system injurious compounds, some of which are extremely poisonous; also, that agreeable, happy emotions generate chemical compounds of nutritious value, which stimulate the cells to manufacture energy.

I have succeeded in entirely eliminating vicious propensities from children with dispositions toward cruelty, stealing or anger. In curing a bad habit I would for every evil tendency, image, or craving existing in the same parts of the brain, create a greater number of the opposite kind of memories and keep them active a greater number of times each day, until the old structures had disappeared and new ones had been formed. This process does not require the assent of the patient any further than to take the course of studies. He may even not desire to abandon a certain practice or habit, but may wish to continue his evil course; yet, by the force of brain-building, that motive can be eliminated.

This system of developments can be applied to regulate the assimilative processes, the diseases of which are dyspepsia, alcoholism, etc. A woman unable to eat fatty or greasy substances, even in the smallest portions, was by this system trained to take them in normal quantities. The alcohol habit, when not engendered by the habitual and excessive use of liquors, can originate through a certain derangement of the stomach and the brain-cells that govern it. Indigestion, accompanied by fermentation of sweets, creates a small amount of alcohol in the stomach. This alcohol produces a stimulating effect which the patient misses when the fermentation is arrested by the alcohol itself, or by a change in the food. The first step toward curing this habit consists in forming another series of brain-structures of the different stages relating to previous experiences, not merely with intoxicants but with foods in general. The creation of at least a hundred times as many morally-functioning cells as there had been immorally-functioning cells will cause the craving for stimulants to disappear. It is possible in three months' time to develop brain-structures which will cause a patient to feel disgust for what he had previously relished and desired.

The late Prentice Mulford says, in one of his pamphlets, that "to think success brings success." Unfortunately, however, such effort has but a limited effect in the usual business life. Aside from lack of training or of knowledge, present defects in business life result from an improper classification of the memories and an erroneous use of mental faculties. The mind is usually filled with disordered, disquieting memories which, as a rule, are accompanied by an equal number of pleasant or unpleasant experiences. Wearisome, unpleasant memories weaken health and do not generate thought energy. Cure is accomplished in expelling these by another crop of wholly pleasant memories, which put the necessary structures of the mind in systematic order and teach the patient how to use the mental faculties.

I have been asked how far this new science is related to phrenology. Phrenology had the misfortune of falsely locating every mental function. For instance, sight was placed near the middle of the eyebrow, whereas its true position is in the back of the head. The absence of all memory-cells predominant in any mental faculty could not be discernible through the skull or scalp, because such absence would not change the cerebral cortex of that part of the brain as much as the tenth of an inch. There is, however, alike in man and animals, a general conformation, not merely of the head but of the entire body, which gives us some knowledge of the mental capacity. This will be obvious to any one who observes the facial angles and other characteristics among monkeys and the lower races of human beings.

These discoveries, by giving to individuals a better use of the mind, open a new epoch in the methods of progress and civilization. It is the mind which creates sciences, arts and institutions —which knows, suffers and enjoys; and it is the mind that must continue to do all that is done. Give to people more mind, and all undertakings will be ameliorated, and better results accomplished. Give them more moral mind, and the evils of society will gradually disappear. If it is possible to give more mentality to people, then at last, through scientific experimentation, we have reached a fundamental law of morals.

If you will remember that it is the mind that thinks, feels, knows, and performs physical labor; that it is the mind that rages, plots, and exercises all propensities, whether moral or immoral—then you will understand my meaning when I say that every act is right which, in its immediate or remote consequences, give us more mind, or a better control and use of the mental faculties; and every act is wrong which, immediately or remotely, produces the opposite result. There can be no other right or wrong. An evil memory promptly antagonizes the functioning of the good memories, slowly poisoning not only the body of which the memory is a part, but memory itself.

A statement made some months ago, by being falsely reported, has done me much harm. I was alleged to declare that sin is pink in color. It is, however, as inaccurate to speak of the color of sin as of the moral qualities of a vacuum. If an evil emotion is dominant, then during that period the respiration contains volatile poisons, which are expelled through the breath and are characteristic of these emotions. By applying chemical reagents I can detect the presence of these poisons, because a precipitate is produced; and this precipitate generally has some color. In the case of grief, for instance, if I use rhodopsin for my reagent, the color will be pinkish. Other reagents will produce other colors.

My researches in brain-building have led to a demonstration of the evil effects of hypnotism. This practice produces a species of congestion of the brain. The pupil in the science of mind-structure who desires to achieve good mental and moral character must avoid hypnotic experiences, under no circumstances permitting himself to be hypnotized—save, perhaps, for some absolutely necessary surgical purpose. Hypnotism tends to vitiate the moral character.

The various methods of mind cure, faith cure, laying on of hands, and similar processes that have come down to us from remote ages, have each some sort of a fundamental verity. One aspect of the truth has been seen, but it is generally combined with many mischievous practices and belief, and is seldom scientifically applied. My experiments prove that the mind activities create the structures which the mind embodies, or manifests. In addition to massage, diet, regulations of surroundings, etc., modern medicine will eventually evolve methods of brain-building to effect cures. Simple belief that you will get well, will, in a measure, produce nutritious products and stimulate the health of the entire body. The indulgence of certain emotional states will do the same. To achieve any certain result, however, the process must begin with the first stages of brain-building and be pursued systematically to the highest stages, in order to create in the brain those structures which govern different portions of the body. This can best be done by the methods I have described.

The value of this new science will be better understood when we remember that mind underlies all sciences, art, and institutions. The mind has produced all our paintings, poems, literatures, languages, architectures, governments, and religions. Your mind is, to you, the most momentous and important fact in the universe; for without your mind, what would be the nniverse and its possibilities to you? Take away your mind, and what would there be left? To your own mind you must always look for guidance. If you can get more mind, or a better regulated mind, you will fundamentally and directly promote all your undertakings. You will be better able to apply whatever knowledge you possess.

Real progress among peoples is the degree of their mental development. To test this statement, imagine progress in civilization which at each step produces less and less mind! To give people more mind is at once to promote all reform and all progress. If evolution did not lead to more mind, it would be retrogression

As my investigations and experiments in the art of mind-building are directly related to psychology, the reader may ask my definition of that term. Psychology is the science of mind. The word comes from the Greek "psycho," meaning soul. The earlier psychologists, being metaphysicians and none of them experimentalists, believed that in their speculations they were dealing with the faculties of the soul. Whether they were or not is not the question now under consideration. The art of mind-building and the art of mind-using, which I have evolved from the data of psychology, I have named "psychurgy."

The experimentalist knows mind only as he finds it manifested in himself and in other living creatures. He believes that this entity cannot exist apart from structure. Mind, however, is not a function of the brain in the same sense as bile is a secretion of the liver. The functioning of the individual organism is but one factor of mind. A more important factor is the fundamental connection of the individual organism with the cosmic environment. Mind may be more than this, but at least it is this. I make no distinction between mind and soul. I do not attempt any definition of mind further than that it is the totality of the sub-conscious and conscious adaptive functions of the organism in interaction with the Cosmos.

Modern psychology began within the last fifty years with Fechner, Helmholtz, Wundt, and their followers. They commenced to measure sensations and times of reaction, to study the effect of diseases upon the brain, and to make investigations of the cerebral cortex through electrical stimulations of those areas and through ablations and excisions thereof. As a result, we have physiological psychology, or psycho-physics.

I shrank from vivisection and regarded the results of Horsley's and Monk's experiments upon brains as somewhat untrustworthy, because, when you remove a portion of the cortex (the outer line of gray matter which covers the cerebrum), you destroy the fibrous and the blood-vessel connections with other brain areas, producing a pathological but not a normal result. In the first part of this interview I described my experiments upon animals by a method which does not require vivisection and which does not produce diseased results.

This brain-building process embodies a number

of successive stages. The first stage consists in enregistering the sense impressions of all the senses, so as to produce sensation-structures. In the new nomenclature, cognizance of a sense impression is called "sensation." The conscious state which we call "perceiving a sense impression" produces a chemical deposition of matter in the brain-cells, and each repetition of that sense-consciousness increases the amount of matter deposited, the result being a sense-memory structure. The refunctioning of that structure constitutes memory.

As soon as all the sensation-structures have been formed in the brain, we can begin the second stage, which consists in causing the child to discriminate between the different sensations previously acquired and to associate them in consciousness, so as to produce what is called an integrant of the second order, or images, the units of which are the sensations of the first stage of brain-building. And so on through thirty or forty successive stages.

This process can be applied up to the period of decrepitude, but it is probable that it can be fully realized only when commenced with infants; and, inasmuch as the germ-cell of the female is directly affected by the nutriment which it gets from the parents' blood, it follows that a proper course of living before conception will directly affect the development of the child. My experiments have demonstrated that every emotion of a false and disagreeable nature produces a poison in the blood and cell tissues. These poisons affect the health of the germ-cells. During pregnancy, life-depressing and unpleasant emotions—grief, anger, sorrow, etc.—will, through the poison generated, affect the development of the fœtus. For this and other reasons brain-building should properly begin a few months before conception.

Out of these researches arose not only a method of mind-building, or mind-embodiment, but also the art of using the mind systematically in original thinking, which art may be suddivided as follows: (1) the art of systematic, originative, conscious mentation; (2) the art of systematic sub-conscious mentation; and (3) the art of systematic originative, co-operative mentation. These arts lead to original thinking, invention and discovery by a systematic training in the use of the intellectual, emotive, and conative lines of mentation, and in each of the mental faculties. The pupil desiring to discover new things in any science has his brain rebuilt with reference to that science. This is the first step. He is then taught whatever knowledge the human race has acquired concerning that subject, and to each of these data he is trained several hours a day, for a few years, to apply each one of his mental faculties.

The rules of this art have been derived from many thousand experiments and observations, and by practical application to myself and pupils. Two men of equal knowledge may study the same phenomena and the same data, and one of them will evolve original ideas and make discoveries, while the other will add nothing to our knowledge of the subject. Now, the mind art will enable the former to do better thinking, and will so train the latter to use his mind that he, also, will make discoveries and originate ideas. At present almost every organic and cosmic law of originative mentation is persistently violated by the investigator.

With the sum of human knowledge in any science classified in the mind; with a rebuilt brain from which evil affections and emotions have been eliminated; and with proper regulation of the body and its surroundings, the pupil commences to practice the art of original thinking somewhat as follows: According to rules which must be learned to be understood, he exercises every one of his thirty or forty mental functions upon each proposition or datum of the science, in order that each faculty may be active a certain number of hours each day. This produces brain-growth in those very parts of the brain which are needed to deal with that subject. As the new growth is acquired, day after day, the sub-conscious functions become stimulated, the cosmical inter-actions of the brain become more vivid, and new ideas dawn as suddenly as lightning illuminates a landscape. New congruities, and generalizations are achieved, and, as a result, a reclassification of that knowledge must soon be made. Then the pupil again applies each mental function to each one of those data until he gets a new growth in those parts of the brain needed for the study of that particular subject. Six months' practice generally quadruples the mental capacity and more than quadruples the number of ideas gained each day. Such ideas must always be tested for truthfulness by observation and experiment in that domain of nature to which they relate.

Then there is the art of regulating the sub-conscious mental functions. At least ninety-eight per cent. of our mental life is sub-conscious. If you try to remember what happened on your tenth birthday, it may be ten minutes before you can recall any incident. What occurs while you are trying to remember? Certainly not conscious processes. The processes of memory are in the subconscious domain.

If you will closely analyze your mental operations you will find that consciousness—conscious thinking—is never a continuous line of consciousness, but a series of conscious data with great intervals of sub-consciousness. We sit, trying to solve some problem, but fail. We rise, walk around, try again, and still fail. Suddenly an idea dawns which leads to the solution of the problem. The sub-conscious processes were at work. We do not volitionally create our thinking. It takes place in us. We are more or less passive recipients. We cannot change the nature of a thought or of a truth, but, we can, as it were, guide the ship by moving the helm. Our mentation is most largely the result of the operation of the cosmic Whole upon us. Annihilate the Cosmos, and our thinking would instantly cease.

Sub-conscious mentation is regulated by maintaining proper conditions of the body and environment, i. e., the forces which affect the body. Co-operative mentation consists in a number of specialists applying the art of conscious mentation to the same subject at the same time. If all the great minds of the human race were trained in this mode of systematic mentation, and if they were to take for their subject the sum of human knowledge, they would achieve an interpretation of the universe which we may call philosophy, using the word as the synthesis of the generalizations of science. The result of each day would be a stepping-stone for the next. And if such minds, trained in these arts of originative mentation, were thus to deal with the whole scope of human knowledge systematically, they would continually eliminate former errors and constantly add new insights and new discoveries to their interpretation of the universe.

Such a perpetual, re-organized philosophy I have called "omnism." This philosophy is the highest generalization that can at any time be achieved by a number of the ablest minds practising co-operative mentation upon the sum of human knowledge. It is not realism, nor idealism, nor monism. It is, of course, a synthesis of all philosophies and branches of knowledge by specially constructed brains, acting according to systematic methods of mentation which begin by eliminating the immoralities in the mind. Such a philosophy could never become a fixed creed or belief.

Mentation is mind in activity. Using the word "psychology" as including all of the sciences of mind, I may further define it by saying that there are six experimental sciences of mentation; and the generalizations which arise from a synthesis of the data from each of these six domains of research constitute psychology proper.

The first of these six domains is comprised by Biologic Psychology. In this realm the investigator experimentally varies the structures of the organisms and the conditions of their environment in order to discover what mentations result from each variation. This includes most of what is called physiological psychology and psychophysics. After many hundreds of experiments in this line I established a new method of research in biologic psychology. It consists in giving organisms new anatomical structures or in taking anatomical structures away from them in order to see what mental activities appear and disappear with the coming and going of these structures. No; I do not vivisect, mutilate or graft! I do it by a rapid process of evolution and retrogression. I evolve the structures of organisms in the process of rapid evolution to higher or more complex structures, or to lower and simpler ones. I raise several million infusoria (animalcules that occur in infusions of decaying substances) in a tank, and then, by gradually increasing heat or cold, or concussions, I destroy all except two or three proved to be the most capable of surviving. These survivors propagate several million more, and, generation after generation, the process is repeated. After about twenty-one months, new structures arise, and I made a note of the concomitant mentations, or adaptive activities which also arise. As a method of psychological research, this is new.

I am organizing a laboratory of subjective biological investigation which will contain a great many new instruments.

I am also organizing a laboratory of subjective biopsychology, with special apparatus never before seen by psychologists. This science varies, one at a time, the environmental conditions of the pupil, and he observes the effect produced upon his own conscious mentations. The moods and intellections are found to vary with the electrostatic potentials—humidity, altitude, etc. I have found that, for successful mentation, it is as necessary to maintain high electrostatic conditions in the student's room as to maintain a healthful temperature. The potentials referred to are the electrical changes in the atmosphere. These electrostatic potentials of the atmosphere change constantly, varying often many million of volts every hour. Every change makes an alteration in your emotions, you secretions, your excretions, and your whole mentation.

I am also starting a third laboratory—sociological psychology. A prominent scientist recently said that this is the first step toward experimental sociology. I will have special apparatus, much of which is now being made. Sociological psychology consists in varying the environment of social groups of living things, such as a bevy of birds, a school of fish, a hive of bees, etc. As we vary the social structure or the environment of a social group, changes take place in the group-activities. This also is a new method of psychological research. I shall have three other laboratories—six in all. There are six methods of research, which include all possible methods of experimenting upon the mind, and these include much more than what is usually called psychological experimentation.

The mind has created all sciences; consequently, they must all be studied as products of mentation. Included in these six studies are all sciences, which will be studied as subdivisions of the science of mind. A synthesis of the generalization of these six sciences, therefore, will be a synthesis not merely of the six psychological departments, but of all the sciences included therein. The synthesis of these sciences constitutes not only Psychology, but Philosophy also.

Just as correlated with the science of chemistry there is an art of chemistry, so with the science of mind there is an art of mind, or mind-art, more properly called Psychurgy. The latter includes the three arts of getting more mind and the three which pertain to its proper use. The arts of getting more mind are those of Brain-building, Character-building and Immorality-curing and Education. The arts of mind-using are those of conscious originative mentation, sub-conscious originative mentation, and co-operative mentation. The syntheses of these six arts constitutes a synthetic mind art, or Psychurgy.

The experiments I have made contradict the conclusions of Weismann and others regarding heredity. They claim we have no proof of a skill, an idiosyncrasy, or a habit acquired during the lifetime of an individual, being transmitted to that person's offspring. They mention circumcision as practised by the Jews generation after generation, asserting that it is not transmitted. The mutilation of a Chinese woman's foot they say is not transmitted. I say it could not be transmitted because the change does not originate in the mind. If I train an animal in the excessive use of some one mental faculty, its germ (or reproductive) cell will be influenced in its nutrition through the parent's changed metabolism, which is produced by the changed character of the mentation. I have trained four generations of guinea-pigs in the use of the visual faculty, and the children of the fourth generation were born with a greater number of brain-cells in the seeing-areas than other guinea-pigs that had not been thus trained. The experiment has been successfully repeated several times, and it demonstrates the transmission of acquired characteristics. I have found in the uni-cellular organisms, i. e., small protoplasmic cells, when they are caused to respond generation after generation to some one stimulus in excess of all other stimuli, that there gradually arise specific anatomical structures produced by the mental activity which responds to that stimulus. In this experiment, the cells which do not respond as readily as others are not destroyed, but are allowed to propagate as freely as the rest; hence the Darwinian factor of "survival of the fittest" is eliminated, i. e., favorable and unfavorable variations do not signify. The conclusion is that mental activity creates in mental organism certain structures transmissible to their offspring.

In regard to heredity and freedom of the will,

I have this to say: We are all conscious of being capable of doing as we please; if we please to do wrong we find ourselves capable thereof, and *vice versa*. If our motive for wrong-doing predominate—if the majority of our effective and emotive states, our appetites and desires, lead us in a certain way and we have enregistered no mental experiences of an opposing character, or at least not enough of them—then it will be our will to do as our motive leads us, i. e., as we choose.

This question of choice and of motive is based upon the character and degree of mind that the person has embodied or inherited. A person can inherit tendencies of growth in certain parts of the brain. His memories of sensations, images, concepts, emotions. and activities must come from experience. If a majority of these memories, relating to a certain object or event, are pleasurable, the person will naturally like it. If a majority of the experiences are un-pleasurable, or evil, he will in the one case not like the object, and in the other he may either like it or dislike it, according as the evil experiences are pleasurable or the reverse. The person's will is the result of the interaction of the totality of his memory-structures relating to any given object or event. It is possible completely to change the dominance of his desires and motives, likes, and dislikes, etc., by enregistering in any part of his brain another series of memories, and, by so doing, you control the will. This is called "auturgy"; it is the art of systematically controlling the will by a process of brain-building and character-building based upon a taxic registration of experiences with the Ego.

The power which is active in the mind to control the will is a centrimmanent force of a cosmical character, omnipersonal, unitary, and the basis of Auturgy.

The Laboratory of Psychology and Psychurgy is now the scene of experiments in these various lines. The Laboratory is growing in completeness, and its purpose is to study the mind scientifically, to diffuse the knowledge thus obtained, to cure immoral dispositions, to train investigators, and to organize research along these lines."

Old and New Phrenology

(A LETTER.)

II
OLD AND NEW PHRENOLOGY.

WASHINGTON, D. C. July, 13, 1896.

EDITOR THE METAPHYSICAL MAGAZINE:

Dear Sir—On page 4 of the July number of The Metaphysical Magazine, the inadvertency and too great brevity of the reporter have made me criticize phrenology in a way that does not correctly represent my attitude toward a domain of research which promises some day to become a science.

In speaking of phrenology I meant the "old" phrenology, not the new; and what I desired the reporter to say was that "the old phrenology had the strange misfortune of incorrectly locating a great many of the functions of the brain, and also of assigning locations to functions and supposed faculties that do not exist in any definitely localized areas" The higher faculties are complex combinations of mental integrants of simple-forms, which simpler memory-structures are distributed all over the brain surface and not confined to any one locality. Thus, when I relate the concept of "orange" with the concept of "nutrition," into the idea that "oranges are nutritious," I am exercising more than one locality of the brain. For example, the above idea requires the activity of the color-areas in the part of the cerebral cortex, of the taste-areas at the base of the cerebrum, of the smell-areas in another part of the base of the cerebrum, of the touch-areas in still another part of the cerebrum, of the speech-motor areas in still another, etc. In like manner the "faculties" named by the old phrenologists "spirituality," "logic," "inventiveness," etc., are exceedingly complex combinations of functions widely scattered, not merely over all areas of the cerebrum, but diversely through the different areas of the six or eight cell-layers of the cortex.

It would have been more accurate also if the reporter had made me say that "the true position of the color-memories is in the cortex of the back part of the cerebrum, in the region of the cuneus," instead of that of "sight." The old phrenologists located color in the region of the forehead, near the outer angle of the eyebrow and a little above it. Modern physiologists and psychologists have positively demonstrated that the color-memories are located in the cerebral cortex at the back of the head, nearly opposite the location assigned by the old phrenologists. Sight is a complex combination of the memory-structures in this area, with other kinds of memory-structures in several other areas.

The old phrenologists assigned a definite location in the forehead to a faculty called "memory." Now, no fact of modern physiology or of psychology has been more clearly established than the fact that there is not a faculty of memory located in any one small area of the brain, but that every area of the brain-cortex has it own memories. Every functioning structure and every conscious experience that can be remembered exists as a memory-structure. In the region of the cuneus, in the back part of the head, are the color-memories; and if that part becomes destroyed by disease those memories are also destroyed; in the first temporal lobes above the ears are the sound-memories; in the region of the "fissure of Rolando" are the muscular motor-memories; and so on. Memories (plural) are in every part of the brain-cortex, and it is not true that memory (singular) has one definite location. I refer to the "Physiology" of Landois and Stirling, to Ladd's "Physiological Psychology," to Foster's "Physiology," to the writings of Ferrier, Munk, Monakow, etc., as well as to my own researches, for abundant proof of these statements, and to modern medical, physiological, and psychological literature in general.

But I do not therefore decry phrenology. These discoveries teach how to improve upon the old art of character-reading, to avoid its mistakes, and to take advantage of the newly discovered truths. Every mental characteristic finds expression in form and feature throughout the whole domain of animal life. Even recent emotional experiences are graphically depicted in the physiognomy, and when such experiences are long continued the "phrenological" features are also affected. There is, therefore, a sound scientific basis for character-reading. The art, in the hands of good practioners, even despite the errors to which I have called attention, has enabled them to make readings of character which could not be the result of guesswork, and their percentage of correct delineations has been far greater than their mistakes. A more accurate knowledge of functional localization in the brain and the discovery of errors in the old phrenology will not injure the art of character-reading, but rather raise it to the level of a scientific art.

Very truly yours,

ELMER GATES.

Psychology and Psychurgy

III

PSYCHOLOGY AND PSYCHURGY.

THE NATURE AND USE OF THE MIND.

In this paper I have thought it well to call attention to the importance of a study of the Science of Mind (Psychurgy).

The word "Mind," as I have herein used it, signifies the totality of the phenomena of Consciousness and includes all that can feel, remember, or adapt acts to ends; and, therefore, it properly includes all of the phenomena of the Intellect, such as sensations, images, concepts, ideas, thoughts, reasonings, introspection, etc. It includes all of the activities of the systemic and organic feelings and of the tender, æsthetic, moral, logical and religious emotions. It includes the whole subject of volition and will; and it includes a study of all of the vital and subconscious processes connected with the the exercise of these functions. It includes affections, tastes, habits, knowledge, conduct and civilization. Whatever thing can feel and adapt acts to ends has mind ; and therefore, the study of the mind includes feeling, memory, and adaptive activity. Psychology, therefore, includes the study, by scientific methods, of our own minds and of the minds of all living organisms, so that we may judge from the facts regarding anatomy, physiological activities, habits, environment, etc., what mind IS, and so that we may learn by a study of minds what organisms ARE.

The definition which I have herein made of the mind is the one I have found most consistent with the general study and practice of Psychurgy, or the Art of Mentation; but the philosophic import of this definition, that mentality includes and is synonymous with vitality, constitutes no necessary part of the science of mind as I desire to teach it, or of the psychurgic art. But it will be necessary for the reader to remember that the meaning which I have herein given to the word "mind" includes all there is of consciousness, together with the functionally associated subconscious processes of the organism; that is, it includes within its scope the psychologic characteristics of the cellular activities. The organs of the body are composed of cells, and these cells can feel stimuli and perform adaptive activities, and as only mind can feel and adapt, it follows that what characterizes the life of a cell is its mind-capacities. If a cell cannot feel and perform adaptive actions, it is dead. I do not attempt to philosophize upon the subject; I prefer to await further knowledge of the mind. It matters not, as far as an understanding of the principles of the art of using the mind are concerned, whether mind includes all there is of vitality or not; or whether there is Mind *and* Matter; or *Spirit*, Mind and Matter; or whether Mind, like number, dimension, motion, and persistence is a property inseparable from matter; or whether there is an energy that manifests as Matter, Mind, Motion, etc. These questions I do not attempt to decide, but the fact remains that it is the mind-like capacity of the cell that constitutes its life, and that it is out of these mind-like functionings of the cells of the body and brain that the conscious processes of the human mind arise; or, if you prefer a different philosophical implication, you may say that it is the judgment-properties of the matter of the body becoming dynamically evolved and accentuated as compared with the space-properties, motion-properties, number-properties, and time-properties of the matter of the body.

Some people have supposed that there is in us a higher kind of intelligence than mental; such, for example, as that of the "soul;" and that, therefore, psychology does not include within its survey all of the phenomena of life. To see the incompleteness of this belief, it will suffice to say, without at present committing myself to either the materialistic or spiritualistic hypotheses, that if the soul has not, or is not, a Mind, then it cannot feel, nor remember, nor know, nor adapt acts to ends. To maintain this position is equivalent to saying that the soul is inanimate. If that which has been called "soul," "spirit," etc., can feel, remember, know, adapt acts to purposive ends, etc., then the scope of psychology includes all such phenomena. Science has experimented upon the mind, but it has not yet, in the same manner, experimented upon the soul, if by "soul" is meant something different from mind. I doubt if it ever pays to theorize or express opinions upon this, or upon any other subject, or to discuss matters in advance of scientific evidence; but it will serve to illustrate my point of view if I may be allowed to say that if there are orders of existence higher than man (and there is no reason why the Universe in its infinite possibilities should not contain them), then, no matter how much higher and greater than man's conceptions these forms may be, and no matter in what unknown states and conditions they may exist, if they can feel and know and act, they must have minds, and thereby they will fall within the survey of psychology. Furthermore, if there is embodied in the whole Cosmic Universe a Supreme Mind in some manner analogous to the way in which mind is embodied in the human organism (and I say it with deep and genuine reverence), then, in studying the phenomena of mind you will, to that extent, become acquainted with the kind of power that lies at the head of Cosmos.

I say, that if there is purposive intelligence at the head of the Universe, and if that which has been called God or the Supreme Being can know, or adapt acts to ends, or if that which has been called the Creator can be conscious, then it must *have* Mind or *be* Mind, and in that case, to learn the laws of consciousness is to learn something about that which rules the whole Cosmic Event throughout all space and duration. Your mind must be, in its own nature, similar unto that cosmic condition in the Universe out of which it came, or of which it is an eternal part. Your mind cannot be in fundamental antagonism and contradiction to the cosmic order out of which it was generated and from which it has directly inherited all of its characteristics; and, therefore, to introspectively and scientifically know the nature and laws of your own mind is to know directly that much of what is the most interesting, mysterious, wonderful, and perhaps the most all-pervading and potent force in the Universe. It is to know in your own consciousness and as consciousness the power that rules life and is life in all worlds and times. If "that, than which there can be nothing greater," has the power to know or to have a purpose, then that power must be due to mind; and in that case, to the extent that you know the mind, just to that extent you know the Universe ontologically. Or if, for the sake of still illustrating a point of view, we assume the opposite belief and contend that there is in the Universe no being higher than man, and that death ends the individual life, then it still follows that the chief subject of study must be the mind, for it is the mind that constitutes the man and is his only guide through life.

From the psychurgic standpoint all sciences should be studied as subdivisions of psychology, and that fact has been to many a puzzling feature. I have often been asked, "Why do you devote so much time and give such prominence to the experimental study of chemistry, physics, botany, zoology, mathematics, history, and the other sciences, when your laboratories are devoted to psychology?" "Why do you study music, metallurgy, microscopy, photography, electricity, and the arts generally, when your work is psychological?" The popular idea is that these subjects have no connection with the study of psychology. The reason why the sciences constitute such a prominent feature in the study of the science of the mind is, that we must study the products of mental activity in order to understand the mental functions which produce these products. It must be obvious that the most wonderful, useful and notable products of the mind's action are these very sciences. Not only are the sciences discovered and known by means of the mind-activities, and by no other way, but each science is a particular mode of mental functioning and comprises a particular kind of mental content. Hence, the sciences offer the best fields for the study of the mind through its products, modes and contents. In order to adapt acts to ends—in order that such a thing as conduct may be possible—the mind must know. It must have a knowledge about the things on which and in the presence of which it acts, as well as a knowledge of the thing (the mind) that does the acting. Without such a knowledge of things outside of the body no adaptive action whatsoever could take place. Now, such a knowledge of things, no matter how meagre, must be a knowledge about some of the natural groups of objects in the universe around us, such as the starry-group (Astronomy), or the plant-group (Botany), or the animal-group (Zoology), or the substance-group (Chemistry), and so on; that is, a normal mind must contain correct knowledge of each taxonomic group of phenomena, and only to the extent that it does possess such knowledge can normal and safe conduct be possible.

The intimate and direct relation of the sciences to the study of the mind must be obvious to any one who will reflect upon this aspect of the subject. In like manner the arts represent what the mind has done in applying knowledge to human uses. It is not enough to discover by means of the intellect a new truth; it is not even enough to feel the beauty and possible utility of such a discovery; the mental process is not completed until that truth which you know, and that beauty which you feel have been rendered concrete and available for human uses by conation, or by that act or series of acts which applies this knowledge and feeling to the good of the human race. The industrial and fine arts represent the utilitarian and æsthetic deeds of the mind and the methods by which the mind applies knowledge and feeling. In the practical study of these arts we come in closest and completest touch with the mind's modes of working. The sciences and arts, are, therefore, from this point of view, properly, subdivisions of the science of psychology.

If it is the mind that creates and discovers every science and art, and if it is in the mind alone which can supply such knowledge to an amelioration of the conditions of life; if it is the mind that builds every house, writes every book, and paints every picture; if it is the mind that suffers and enjoys; then it follows that a knowledge of how to regulate the functions of the mind so as to achieve results more economical and more truthful, will rank first in importance in the knowledge to which the human race has been paying attention.

It will be impossible to fully describe this Art in a single paper. I will very briefly describe the first step, which consists, among other things, in the complete inductive mastery of some one science by the psychurgic method. First of all, each one of the nine kinds of sensory functionings, such as touch, pressure, warmth, cold, muscular feeling, taste, smell, seeing and hearing, are trained for several months, until the sensitiveness and accuracy have been increased from five to ten times! * These senses are the instruments of observation by which all knowledge is acquired.† If a person had been born without any of the senses he could never have known of the existence of a single object, and knowledge and conduct would have been impossible to him.

After this training of the senses the pupil should be taken into a building wherein have been placed, in classific groups, every object and piece of apparatus known to some one science, so that every phenomenon of that science might be shown to him, in taxonomic order. The second step consists in giving the pupil correct images of every object belonging to that science; then in causing the pupil to classify these images into naturally-related groups, for the purpose of forming concepts of such groups. The next step consists in experimentally discovering the relations which exist in nature between the objects for which the pupil has concepts; and thus arise ideas. The pupil is then taught how to discover truths common to two or more such ideas, and thus arise thoughts of the first order or laws of the first

---

* I have proof of this.

† Knowledge of physical objects and their relations, rather, we should say. "Subjects" and "Principles" are matters of knowledge, but are not recognizable by the senses.—ED.

degree of generalization. The generalization of thoughts of the first order produces thoughts of the second order, where most sciences end.

In thus acquiring psychologic data belonging to any science the pupil avoids learning any theories, hypotheses or speculations! He learns the science by first-hand observation and acquires the sum total of the knowledge relating to that group of phenomena. By this means he observes that there are no other kinds of knowledge about phenomena than the sensations, images, concepts, ideas and thoughts which he may inductively derive from a study of such objects. This puts normal content in the mind. The pupil is next taught conceptual reasoning, and ideative reasoning, and thinking reasoning; and then made to introspect all of these processes while they are taking place; this finishes the intellectual acquisition of that science (The concomitant emotional or moral training and the concomitant volitional training I will not now describe).

Having mastered this science, the pupil then re-images each one of the images belonging to that science, and thus causes certain parts of the brain to grow stronger and increases the imagining speed from five to ten times.* He then re-concept-

---
* I have proof of this.

uates the concepts, re-ideates the ideas, re-thinks the thoughts, and this increases the speed and the accuracy of each of these functions. He practices the three kinds of reasoning and introspection, and thus learns for the first time in the history of education to use each one of the intellectual functions independently of the others! He increases the speed of his mental activity from five to ten times! He likewise increases the accuracy of the process. He wastes no time in theory and hypothesis. Each incorrect image, each false idea, misleads the whole mentative functioning and vitiates every conclusion that may be formed. Having thus mastered the normal content of one science, having acquired skill in using each one of the intellectual processes, the pupil is then taught to apply this knowledge and skill to the art of invention and discovery, according to methods that cannot now be described

The object of this mentative art is to discover Truth and apply it to the betterment of life. This is the whole process and scope of evolution, and it involves the getting of more mind at each step. The getting of less mind would not be evolution; hence, every act which give us more mind is right, and every act which gives us less mind is wrong. There is no other kind of knowledge about the universe than just such a knowledge as I have described. A knowledge of one science, however does not suffice. Each one of the natural sciences must thus be learned, to make up a perfectly normal mind.

My plea is for the study of the sciences according to this method, so that by basing our mental operations upon verified truth, without an admixture of speculation, we may the more certainly achieve more and more truth. And it is in the Religion of Truth that I have perfect confidence; I have but little confidence in theory, and speculation, and philosophy. Generally their postulates have been wholly or partly wrong. But truth itself would be of no value were it not for the mind which may learn to apply this truth. Hence, progress resolves itself into a question of the amount of mind which we have and into ways of using the mind. Psychology has, pointed out the feasibility of an art of promoting and regulating the use of the mind in discovery, in invention, and in right living, and the development of this art, which I have called Psychurgy, shows that we can systematize the hitherto undirected mental functions of talent and genius, and reduce to scientific rule the haphazard efforts of the mind in discovering Truth. Investigators and thinkers have hitherto violated almost every bodily, environmental and psychologic condition conducive to the best mental functioning, and for some unaccountable reason the human race has studied almost every subject except how best to use that mind which makes all such studies possible. There is a correct way of acquiring scientific data; there is a correct way of regulating bodily and environmental conditions so as to conserve organic energy and promote mental functioning; and the development of such an art of Mentation is destined to exert an important influence upon any individual life and through that upon the life of the race.

You did not create your own consciousness; you did not form the nature and capacities of your own mind; it had its own immanent nature when you first became aware of consciousness, and out of it has grown the total sum of your experiences and possibilities. The wonder of consciousness taking place within us according to its own eternal laws, and in obedience to its own cosmical nature, may well profoundly amaze and astound us. It is an ever-present mystery and wonder towards which our aspirations may lead us to an increasing knowledge, not only of the mind, but of the things in the presence of which it exists.

I regard Mind with as much reverence as I have ever regarded the infinite Cosmic Universe out of which all mind is born. With overwhelming awe I meditate upon the star-studded expanse, with systems of worlds floating therein, and doubtless filled with life—systems of worlds that in presence of Eternity come and go like bubbles upon the stream, but it is with still deeper awe and reverence that I turn to that Awareness in me which is conscious of every passing conscious state; which observes critically, and with absolute justice, the phenomena of mind as they are imperfectly and partially exhibited to me in my consciousness; and I feel that if there be an intelligent purpose or Consciousness at the head of that which has eternally filled unlimited space, then to the extent that I learn the truth about mind, to that extent I become acquainted with the power that is regnant in nature. Whatever of purpose or plan there is in the whole or in any part of the universe, must be due to mind, and whatever you and I may achieve for self or others must be due to the activity of the mind functioning in us; and this mind which takes place in us, and of which we become aware, is as much a cosmical process as is the flow of the tides or the evolution of the universe. A knowledge of your own mind and how best to use it is your only possible guide, for what can never come to your consciousness can never be a part of you or for you. Mind is the path to the goal of all possibilities. This is the age of the apotheosis of Mind.

Occult, Metaphysical

AND

Theosophical Books.

PUBLISHED AND FOR SALE BY

Theosophical Society
PUBLISHING DEPT.

244 LENOX AVENUE,   NEW YORK, N. Y.

FULL CATALOGUE ON APPLICATION.
BOOKS SENT POSTPAID ON RECEIPT OF PRICE.

BIBLE TESTIMONY TO THEOSOPHIC TRUTH. Paper, 10c.
   The writer cites a number of passages from the Bible which prove that it supports the Theosophic Doctrines of Karma and Reincarnation.

BLAVATSKY, H. P.
——— VOICE OF THE SILENCE. Cloth, 50c; leather, 75c.
   The "Voice of the Silence" is derived from the "Book of the Golden Precepts," one of the works put into the hands of mystic students in the East.
   To the diligent searcher this book opens up a view of the future awaiting the soul, and shows the successive stages which the soul must pass through on its way to enlightenment and final perfection.

COLLINS, (MABEL).
——— LIGHT ON THE PATH. Cloth, 50c.; flexible leather, gilt side stamp, round corners, red edges, 75c.
   This beautiful classic contains the original notes of the author as well as the comments from "Lucifer," and the instructive essay on "Karma" that appeared in the original edition, but which has been omitted from some of the later ones.

——— THE IDYLL OF THE WHITE LOTUS. Cloth, $1.00.
   A truly inspiring book, containing a story which has been told in all ages and among every people. It is the tragedy of the Soul. Attracted by Desire, it stoops to sin; brought to itself by suffering, it turns for help to the redeeming Spirit within, and in the final sacrifice achieves its apotheosis and sheds a blessing on mankind.

DHOLE'S VEDANTA SERIES.
——— THE PANCHADASI. From the Sanskrit, with annotations. Two volumes in one. Cloth, $2.50.
   Printed in Calcutta.
   An encyclopedia of spiritual training. Panchadasi is the greatest and most complete work on the Vedanta Philosophy. A complete key to the science of man, his relation to the universe, and his ultimate destiny.

DUNKLEY, (MAUDE).
——— NATURE'S ALLEGORIES. Gilt top; cloth, 75c.
   A beautiful book, especially for young people, expressive of the idea of intelligence in plant life. It is filled with quaint conceits,

beautiful conceptions, through which is breathed the spirit of love and peace.

FLAGG, (WILLIAM J.)
—— YOGA, OR TRANSFORMATION. $3.00.

A faithful representation of the various religious dogmas concerning the soul and its destiny, and embracing the Akkadian, Hindu, Taoist, Egyptian, Hebrew, Christian, Greek, Mohammedan, Japanese and other systems of Magic. This book is an evidence of the great research and study of the author, setting forth as it does the methods adopted by the different religious systems in the attainment of "Yoga" or Union with the Divine. Transformation from the animal-man to the God-man.

FULLERTON, (ALEXANDER).
—— INDIANAPOLIS LETTERS ON THEOSOPHY. Paper, 10c.
—— WILKESBARRE LETTERS ON THEOSOPHY. Paper, 10c.

These two little books contain a series of articles dealing with Elementary Theosophy. They are written in a clear and lucid style and should be in the hands of every beginner.

HARDING, (BURCHAM).
—— BROTHERHOOD, NATURE'S LAW. Cloth, 40c.

This is one of the best books on elementary Theosophy; it is written in a clear and comprehensive style, and just the book for the beginner. Every one can find in it the basis for right conduct, which is convincing to the mind. At the end of each chapter is a series of questions, the answers to which are to be found in that chapter.

HARTMANN, M.D. (FRANZ).
—— MAGIC, WHITE AND BLACK.
Cloth, gilt top, gold side stamp, $2.00.

A very popular book on this profoundly interesting subject. The well-known writer has treated it in a remarkably clear style, which accounts for the numerous editions which have been brought out, all of which have been quickly disposed of.

—— PARACELSUS. Cloth, $2.00.

An extract and translation from his rare and extensive works and from some unpublished manuscripts. This great Occultist was one of the advanced thinkers of his age, whom Virchow admitted to be the father of modern medicine. A fine edition.

JACOLLIOT, (LOUIS).
—— OCCULT SCIENCE IN INDIA and among the Ancients, with an account of their Mystic Initiations and the History of Spiritism. Cloth, $2.50.

An unbiased account of the result of researches, pursued for many years, in the subject of occult science and the practices of the initiated. Being neither an advocate of these beliefs, nor the opposite, the author sets forth things as he saw them with his own eyes and records faithfully such explanations as were received by him. A valuable addition to every library.

JOHNSON, (ETHELBERT).
—— THE ALTAR IN THE WILDERNESS. Cloth, 50c.; paper, 25c.

This is an attempt to interpret man's seven spiritual ages, or seven well defined spiritual experiences, which every soul is obliged to undergo in the course of its higher evolution. The book is remarkable for the beautiful and easy manner in which this most difficult subject is treated. It is a most valuable little book and will be an ornament to every theosophical library.

JOHNSTON, M.R.A.S. (CHARLES).
—— THE MEMORY OF PAST BIRTHS. Paper, 25c.; cloth, 50c.

In this charming work is explained the theory of rebirth and the operations of the mind in the act of memory, according to Eastern doctrines, with rules for exercising the same so as to recollect what lies back of the present consciousness.

This book enjoys a wide circulation.

—— KARMA: WISDOM AND WORKS. Paper, 35c.

A lucid and comprehensive exposition of one of the fundamental teachings of Theosophy based upon the author's translation from the original Sanskrit.

The writings of this author are well known for the brilliant and scholarly manner in which they are treated.

JUDGE, (WM. Q.).
—— THE BHAGAVAD-GITA.
Pocket size, flexible leather, side stamps, gilt edges, 75c.

In the "Bhagavad-Gita" or "The Book of Devotion" is represented the conversation between the Personal Self and the Divine Consciousness in Man. In it is set forth the Path of Duty, the right performance of Action, and final Union with the Divine. The "Bhagavad-Gita" has been studied by the philosophers of all ages.

——— OCEAN OF THEOSOPHY. With portrait of the author.
154 pages, paper, 35c.; cloth, side stamp, gilt top, 50c.
Written in an easy and popular style, this book gives a clear and systematic exposition of Theosophy, unequalled by any other introductory work. In a small compass it conveys a surprising amount of curious and valuable information.
It is well suited for propaganda work.
——— CULTURE OF CONCENTRATION, Of Occult Powers and Their Acquirement. 10c.
A valuable treatise.

LELAND, (CHARLES G.).
——— HAVE YOU A STRONG WILL, or how to develop and strengthen will-power, memory, or any other faculty or attribute of the mind. 12 mo., cloth, $1.25.
The system advocated is in perfect harmony with the line of thought based upon Eastern Psychology. A very practical book.

MULLER, (MAX).
——— SELECTIONS FROM BUDDHA. Cloth, gilt top, 75c.
Extracts from one of the Books of the East, known as the "Life of Buddha." These selections are passages of an ethical and philosophical character, and are the flower of the divine and ennobling teachings of the light of Asia.

NIEMAND, (JASPER).
——— LETTERS THAT HAVE HELPED ME.
Light cloth, with side stamp, 50c.
"Every statement in them is a statement of law. They point to causes of which life is an effect; that life arising from the Spirit in Nature, and which we must understand as it is manifested within us before we can advance on the Path." A book of great value to the disciple.

ORCUTT, (H. E.).
——— EMPIRE OF THE INVISIBLE. 75c.
A crisp, lucid and interesting account of the after-death states of suicides as narrated by some of them. The reader will smile, pity or sympathize with such. Every page of interest.

PARANANDA, (SRI).
——— ST. MATTHEW, COMMENTARY ON. $2.00.
——— ST. JOHN, AN EASTERN EXPOSITION OF. $2.00.
These are two most remarkable books, being an interpretation of

two of the Christian Gospels by the light of the spiritual experience of those who are known in India as Jivan-muktas, showing that these Gospels, when rightly understood, are in perfect harmony with the teachings of the Vedanta philosophy of India.

The author is a Tamil of high attainments and sound culture in the learning of both the East and West; for many years the representative of his race in the Legislative Council of Ceylon and now the Solicitor General of the Crown in that island.

PICTON, (NINA).

——— THE PANORAMA OF SLEEP: Soul and Symbol.

Illus., cloth, $1.00.

Sixteen symbolic dreams, experienced by the writer, are recounted in beautiful language. The teaching is uplifting and inspiring and easily understood. Artistic illustrations add to the value of the book.

PRYSE, (JAMES M.).

——— REINCARNATION IN THE NEW TESTAMENT.

Paper, 35c.; cloth, 60c.

This work presents the doctrine of Reincarnation as it was taught by Jesus and his disciples. In the light of this book, many of the "dark sayings" throughout the New Testament become lucid and full of meaning; one cannot fully understand the wonderful significance of many of these passages without a knowledge of Reincarnation as applied thereto.

——— THE SERMON ON THE MOUNT and other extracts from the New Testament.

86 pages, wide margins; paper, 35c.; cloth, 60c.

A verbatim translation from the Greek, with notes on the Mystical or Arcane Sense.

Contains "The Sermon on the Mount," "The Coming of the Christos," "The True Path of Power," "A Letter of Iakobas," "A Letter of Ioudas," "The Service of Right Conduct."

This book is of special interest to students of Christian Mysticism and the Occultism of the Bible.

THEOSOPHY, OUTLINE OF. Reprinted from the International Encyclopaedia, 1904. 5c.

WALKER, (E. D.).

——— REINCARNATION (unabridged edition). 350 pages, cloth, $1.50.

A lucid explanation of the subject, as well as the conscientious mention of Western objections, with numerous quotations from Western poems and prose writings upon the teaching.

Much interesting and valuable information is given regarding Reincarnation among the ancients, in the Bible, in early and present day Christianity, etc. Everybody interested in religion should possess this book.

WILDER, M. D., (ALEXANDER).
——— "THE SOUL." 10c.

An excellent treatise on the all-important question, "What is Man, Whence and Whither?"

CPSIA information can be obtained at www.ICGtesting.com
229676LV00012B/212/P

Made in the USA
Columbia, SC
14 May 2020

II

SANCTIFYING PREGNANCY

In the light of the Joyful Mysteries of the Rosary

Margaret Place

Sanctifying Pregnancy
by Margaret Place

Retreat Box Press

This is a reprint of this classic work, faithful to the original, with minor adjustments to formatting. This work is in the public domain.

Cover art: Detail von: Antependium, Straßburg um 1410; Wolle, Leinen, Seide; Museum für Angewandte Kunst Frankfurt am Main, Inv. Nr. 6810. Public domain.

Nihil obstat:
John Eidenschink, O.S.B., J.C.D.,
Censor deputatus.

Imprimi potest:
✠ Baldwin Dworschak, O.S.B., D.D.,
Abbot of St. John's Abbey.

Imprimatur:
✠ Peter W. Bartholome, D.D.,
Bishop of St. Cloud. June 25, 1954.

Foreword

This booklet stands in striking contrast to much that one sees in print on the subject of childbearing and motherhood in the secularized civilizations of our day. In its pages the child is not declared "unwanted." Nor are the tasks of the mother in any way played down.

To the contrary, the child is set forth for all that God meant him to be, and the role of mother is shown with all the beauty that the light of another world reflects upon her. Its pages are replete with Christian gems of thought that cannot but inspire the reader with a profound sense of the glory and dignity of motherhood as planned by God and as viewed by the Church.

A particularly happy feature of the booklet is the arrangement of its content under the five Joyful Mysteries of the Rosary. As a result there is a constant reference to the incidents in the life of the Mother of God. This cannot but encourage and console the Christian mother in her tasks. It will give both her and mothers-to-be the profound sense of respect for the high ideals of Christian motherhood that alone is becoming the true child of Mary.

Furthermore, it will prepare expectant mothers fully to appreciate the meaning of the following words which the minister of Holy Mother Church will say over her in the Blessing after Childbirth:

> *"Almighty, everlasting God, who by the child-bearing of the Blessed Virgin Mary, hast for Thy faithful turned the pains of child-bearing into joy, look with kindness on this Thy servant, who comes rejoicing to Thy holy temple to give thanks to Thee, and grant that after this life she and her child may, by the merits and intercession of the Blessed Virgin Mary, attain to the joys of everlasting life. Through Christ our Lord."*

The publication is a timely one, and deserves to be most widely circulated. Those who peruse it are certain to be influenced by it. The more widely it will be read, the more will it contribute to the building of a better and more Christian world.

Rev. Edgar Schmiedeler, O.S.B., Ph.D.
Director, Family Life Bureau, N.C.W.C.

INTRODUCTION

Much is being written in the press of today on "Motherhood." Almost every issue of the typical "woman's magazine" has at least one article on the subject.

Although these articles range from popularly scientific treatises on childbirth or prenatal care to frivolous advice on the expectant mother's wardrobe, they have for the most part one thing in common—their only concern is with the purely bodily or biological aspects of pregnancy. Rarely does one find a single hint or suggestion of the fact that, besides its purely physical character, the period of approaching motherhood is above all else a time of spiritual awakening and maturing.

Even our Catholic press, which wages such a relentless fight against the evils of birth control, might offer us more of a positive nature on the subject.

Perhaps it is because no one who has not herself sensed this unity with God which comes with motherhood can speak of it, yet it is natural that Christian mothers should be reluctant to reveal so sacred an experience. Today, however, when Satan's sales-ladies roam the country and are seconded by the newspapers, the radio, the women's magazines, even the charming women in the next apartment—all preaching the advantages of birth control and planned parenthood—it is time we speak our hearts.

Our young women should be encouraged to think of pregnancy not as nine months of shapeless clothes, swollen feet, in a word, a period which must be endured—but rather as nine months of very close, beautiful kinship with Almighty God. When one realizes she is to be a mother, what new meaning dawns in that oft repeated catechism question, "Where is God?" She knows that God has indeed been very close to her, that He has breathed an immortal soul into the minute particle of life she now carries beneath her heart. She cannot feel other than close to Him!

When she understands that she is sharing with God some small part of His great work of creation, then she is able to see

that she, too, must accept a small part of His cross in the work of Redemption. That is done by willingly and cheerfully accepting the sacrifice, discomfort, and even suffering that her pregnancy makes necessary.

For many a girl, it may be the first time she has had to deny herself for the sake of another. Self-denial is not easy, yet it brings great compensation when accepted for love.

By meditating on the Joyful Mysteries of the Rosary in the following chapters, let us seek to discover how the period of pregnancy can be sanctified by patterning it on that of the Mother of mothers—the Blessed Virgin Mary.

First Mystery
The Annunciation
YOUR VOCATION IN LIFE

The last chapters of The Seven Story Mountain by Thomas Merton gives us a fascinating account of daily life in a Trappist monastery. For many weeks this book, which is an autobiographical account of a soul's search for contentment, headed the best seller lists. The world was puzzled to learn from it that these men, who through the centuries have denied themselves many legitimate pleasures, have known in fullest measure the only true happiness life can offer.

One reviewer stated that he found it more than interesting because it dealt "not with what happens to a man, but with what happens inside him — that is, inside his soul."

Perhaps this seems a far cry from our original subject. It is indeed a great distance in every sense of the word from the quiet of Gethsemani Abbey to your own fireside; but, sometimes by stepping back a little we face a problem from a new angle and thus gain a clearer perception of it.

Just as Thomas Merton discerned that God had a very definite plan for him which led him through many adventures to the peaceful life of a Trappist — so too, God has a plan for you. The fact is that your being pregnant, your raising a family, is the means God is giving you to save your soul and to assist in the spread of His kingdom. Even at this moment He is looking with favor and love upon the child you bear within you because it is His "son" by creation and will be much more so by the grace of Baptism which is in store for him.

Motherhood is a vocation just as truly as is Thomas Merton's way of life. But like any other vocation, it requires patience, perseverance, and a willingness to serve.

Perhaps you, like many other girls, have not thought of marriage and motherhood in this serious light. Yet it must be so

5

thought of if you are to be a happy and holy mother — and you wish to be both. Now in these months of "shadow" after the honeymoon, you will have time to think and pray and prepare yourself. You will have to exercise some self-discipline, certainly; but love will make it worth doing.

It follows, then, that when the doctor tells you, "no sweets, no salt" or whatever other advice fits your particular needs, you will not assume the air of a "martyr to duty" and make life miserable for yourself and all around you; on the contrary you will have every reason to be happy! Think each day that you and God are working together on a wonderful project. Be proud of the fact that your body has become a sanctuary in which you are sheltering and nurturing an immortal soul.

Your pregnancy is a real privilege which many women have been denied. Do not feel that your reward comes only at the end, with the birth of your child; rather, it is with you constantly if you live each day as Mary lived it. Naturally you will live in joyful anticipation, but all through the nine months, cherish each day of this very close relationship with God.

For the woman who is with child, the Rosary should take on a new and intimate meaning—for in a very small and humble way she is sharing some of Mary's experiences.

God could have chosen to send His divine Son into this world in many ways; but instead He chose to have Him begin life just as all mankind — cradled beneath the heart of a woman. Indeed in Mary, not only motherhood, but pregnancy was sanctified for all time. To Mary alone was given the singular privilege of being the Mother of the Son of God, but all Catholic mothers have the dignity of being mothers of the sons of God.

Why not dedicate, then, in a special manner these months of your life to Mary? As you go about your home performing the routine tasks that now, perhaps, seem so burdensome, remember that Mary kept house for Joseph during her months of waiting. Turn to her for a philosophy of life. Her beautiful words of joy in the Magnificat—sung in thankful recognition for carrying Christ in her womb—should become a part of your daily prayer during your months of waiting.

The Magnificat

My soul magnifies the Lord, *
and my spirit rejoices in God my Savior,
Because he has regarded the lowliness of his handmaid, *
for, behold, henceforth all generations shall call me blessed,
Because he who is mighty has done great things for me, *
and holy is his name;
And for generation upon generation in his mercy, to those who fear him.
He has shown might with his arm;
he has scattered the proud in the conceit of their heart.
He has put down the mighty from their thrones and has exalted the lowly.
He has filled the hungry with good things * and the rich he has sent away empty.
He has given help to Israel, his servant, * mindful of his mercy
Even as he promised to our fathers— *
toward Abraham and his descendants forever.

(Luke 1:46-55)

Another and very important means of grace for the expectant mother is the Church's official blessing of a woman in pregnancy. *The complete text of the blessing is given on page 31.*

Expectant mothers should ask their pastors for this blessing, and should also read and meditate on it often during this time, especially when the time of birth draws near. It will be a great source of comfort to an expectant mother to be reminded how tenderly and solicitously Holy Mother Church thinks of and prays for her.

Since this blessing is little known to many Catholic women, an excellent project for a parish woman's organization would be to acquaint more women with it. Possibly they could arrange to have it administered following one of the regularly scheduled evening services, preferably on or near one of the feasts commemorating Our Lady's Maternity—such as the

Annunciation, March 25; the Visitation, July 2; the Maternity of Mary, October 11; the Expectation, December 18; the Nativity, December 25; or the Purification, February 2.

Over and above the blessing it would bestow, it would awaken in women a real awareness of the spiritual significance of motherhood.

Think, too, of its fine effect on the young girls who might happen to be present. Many of them grow into womanhood and even marry with little understanding of the dignity of bearing a child. For many of them, the mannequin look, the sleek line, is their ideal. They worship at the altar of GLAMOUR. We should do all in our power to instill a Christian attitude on this subject from the days of early adolescence.

Second Mystery
The Visitation
THE AWAKENING

About midway through your pregnancy you have the privilege of experiencing another of God's miracles. The tiny creature you have nurtured for four and a half or five months of life, has grown and developed to a point where movement is possible, and is now making its first faint stirrings.

This is, indeed, a very important milestone in your period of approaching motherhood. The child is growing. It needs more room—the pretty dresses, the smartly tailored suits in your wardrobe must be laid aside. But just as surely as your waistline expands, so too, will the abundance of grace within your heart, if all this is offered to Jesus through Mary.

At this point in your pregnancy it might be well to recall that Our Lord's first miracle, while on earth, was actually performed while He was still in His Mother's womb. As the Gospel tells us: "Now in those days Mary arose and went with haste into the hill country to a town of Juda. And she entered the house of Zachary and saluted Elizabeth. And it came to pass, when Elizabeth heard the greeting of Mary, that the babe in her womb leapt. And Elizabeth was filled with the Holy Spirit, and cried out with a loud voice saying: Blessed art thou among women and blessed is the fruit of thy womb!"

Mary's journey to visit Elizabeth when she learned that Elizabeth was to become a mother shows not only how solicitous she was for her cousin's welfare, but also her natural desire to share the joy of her own approaching motherhood with one whose life-time of prayer for the gift of a child in her womb had at last been answered. Isn't it only reasonable, then, to assume that she takes a personal interest also in you, especially if you are reverent and humble as Elizabeth must have been?

Turn to her often, then, during the months to come, not only for consolation and for help, but for the sharing of your joy:

9

for Mary of the Visitation is essentially a joyful Mary. As your baby's movements within you make you conscious of its presence, say the Memorare:

> *Remember, O most gracious Virgin Mary, that never was it known that anyone who fled to thy protection, implored thy help, and sought thy intercession, was left unaided. Inspired with this confidence, I fly unto thee, O Virgin of Virgins, my Mother! To thee I come, before thee I stand, sinful and sorrowful. O Mother of the Word incarnate, despise not my petitions, but in thy mercy hear and answer me. Amen.*

If you do not already know this beautiful prayer from memory, have several copies about your home —perhaps one in the kitchen, one near the corner where you iron, one on your light stand—until the words come readily to mind. Then, when that tiny hand or foot moves within you wherever you are— riding on a bus, waiting on the doctor's examining table, or even being aroused from sleep by it—your heart will turn instinctively to Mary. You will put all your trust in her, confident that she will not fail you.

At this time it is important for you to follow the advice the doctor gives you to insure your own health and that of your child. Put aside your personal aversions to certain foods if he claims they are essential.

If he advocates moderate exercise, take it. Why not walk over to morning Mass instead of taking an aimless stroll? Couldn't it be within the realm of the possible that just as your child's bodily health is affected by your pre-natal diet, so too, your unborn child's spiritual conditioning may begin long before birth? What a rich heritage the baby has whose mother frequently receives Our Lord in Holy Communion and keeps close to Our Lady while her child grows within her!

Third Mystery
The Nativity
THE BIRTH OF YOUR CHILD

All through the months of your pregnancy your probable date of delivery stands out and looms ahead of you as the big coming event. All else is subordinate to this, and rightly so. Everything is mentally dated B.B.C. (before baby comes) or A.B.C. (after baby comes). The layette you are preparing, the crib your husband is painting, the frilly white curtains—all must be in readiness by this magic date.

But stop now for a minute, and think, are you so completely concerned in making these material preparations that you have lost sight of the deep spiritual significance of the main event? Are you preparing for it as many thoughtless people prepare for Christmas—with Rudolph the reindeer, Frosty the Snowman, tinsel and glitter—but no Christ Child?

Bearing a child is truly a holy act if it is done in cooperation with God. It seems only reasonable then that much of your preparation should be of a spiritual nature. At least you should think through the situation and try to formulate some Christ-like attitudes toward the day or hours preceding the delivery of your child.

Perhaps the first thing you should remember is that frequently the baby is not born on the exact day or date you plan. Therefore, if your due date arrives and you experience none of the physical symptoms your physician has told you to look for, BE PATIENT! In most cases, medical men tell us it simply means that your baby has not come to term. In other words, it needs a few more days or possibly a week or two more of tender, loving care within your body before it is ready to start life on its own.

If you think of it in these terms—difficult as the added days may be—you will not fuss or fume to be relieved of your burden. You have waited nine months, surely you can wait a little longer when you realize it may mean a much better start in

11

life for your baby. Think: God is giving you a few more days to be completely ready for the birth of your child.

Relax, take things a little easier, pray your rosary more devoutly. The Church urges us to prepare for all the important events of our life by prayer. Remember the retreat you made before the reception of First Holy Communion and before receiving the sacrament of Confirmation. An actual retreat at this time is out of the question, but you could enter into the spirit of one—by receiving the sacraments with your husband more frequently during these final days of waiting, by saying a few extra prayers together, and perhaps by some spiritual reading and meditation.

Certainly, this is a more Christ-like way of spending the final days of your confinement than in bitterness, complaining, and self-pity—which in the end will only leave you tired out and exhausted.

The last days before the birth of our Blessed Lord were trying and difficult for Mary, His Mother. She was forced to make the long and arduous journey from Nazareth to Bethlehem with her husband, riding a donkey by day, camping with the caravan by night. She understands your feelings and your problems. Ask her during these last days to help you.

Once you realize that your baby is on its way—don't get panicky! A few contractions simply mean that labor is beginning. It is generally a rather slow process with the first baby. Call your physician and follow his instructions.

If it can be arranged, plan ahead so that your husband will be able to take you to the hospital and stay with you during the hours to come. The modern trend is toward welcoming husbands in the labor rooms. It is his privilege to be with you. If he realizes how very important it is for you to re-main relaxed and reassured at this time, he will gladly follow the suggestions offered by the sisters and nurses in charge of the floor. Those big hands of his which you admired throwing forward passes on the football field, or engaged in some other equally masculine activity, will prove equally proficient at massaging the tired muscles of your back.

Don't shut him out of your life at this time when you really need him. Let him know that his presence is a real help to you. Psychologists tell us that this will bring you closer together than a second honeymoon in Hawaii.

As time progresses, keep your rosary in your hand. The feel of the beads between your fingers will do much to relax you. The modern theory of childbirth is that the more completely relaxed you are during this first stage of labour when the womb is dilating (in other words, when nature is slowly opening the door of the little room where your child has lived), the less discomfort you will feel.

The very words of the Hail Mary and Our Father, said slowly and fervently, will strengthen you and give you faith. For when you say,

Our Father, Who art in heaven,
hallowed be Thy Name:
you are expressing your trust in God who created the infant you are at this moment bringing into the world and who is allowing you in a very humble way to share with Him the joys of creation.

Thy kingdom come.
Realize that this child you are bearing, after it is baptized, will add one more precious soul to God's kingdom.

Thy will be done on earth
as it is in heaven.
Look at your crucifix as you say this part of the prayer. Have faith that the good God who hung for, three hours on the cross will see you through this very natural, beautiful—but sometimes trying—experience, and will give you the patience to do His will now at this moment and during the hours ahead.

Give us this day our daily bread.
Ask our Lord to give you the strength and courage you need for this delivery. Ask Him to watch over your baby, to guard and guide it on its journey into this world.

And forgive us our trespasses
as we forgive those who trespass against us.
Beg forgiveness for the sins of your past life and offer all your discomfort at this moment in atonement for them. Tell our

13

Blessed Lord how very much you wish to start life anew as you assume your new role in life—that of a mother.

And lead us not into temptation
but deliver us from all evil.

Pray that the good God who blessed motherhood for all time by preserving His own Mother free from all sin, will help you and all mothers to overcome temptation—especially, at the moment, the temptations of fear, discouragement, and impatience; and that He will make you strong and worthy of the wonderful title of Christian Mother.

As the hour draws near for the birth of your child, the tempo of the work increases. You will be taken to the delivery room where a whole group has gathered—your own physician, the sister in charge of the floor, the nurses, the anaesthetist. They are all present for just one purpose: to assist you at the delivery of your child. All have been trained to work together as a team. They have gone through this scene many times—only you, the leading lady change with each delivery.

Try to cooperate with their suggestions and requests; it will make things easier for you and better for the baby. Hard work and perseverance are expected of you at this stage. You will hear them say, "Work harder," "Keep working," "Now push once again," until you think these words will be indelibly written in your memory.

All this is a part of God's plan. It is His wonderful way of bringing a new life into the world.

> *"A woman*
> *About to give birth has sorrow*
> *Because her hour has come.*
> *But when she has brought forth the child,*
> *She no longer remembers the anguish*
> *For her joy*
> *That a man is born into the world."*

How true indeed were those words of our Lord! What joy will overflow your heart when you hear the wondrous cry of your new-born child. All else is indeed forgotten when you look

for the first time at this beautiful creature which you have earned the right to call your own child. How happy you and your husband will be when you receive into your arms this precious bundle—a part of you, a part of him—a soul fresh from the hand of Almighty God.

All true love tends to be creative, it seeks an outward expression of its overflowing. This child is an expression of your love for one another, and through it God has truly blessed you by giving you the privilege of parenthood.

Fourth Mystery
Presenting Jesus in the Temple
WE PREPARE FOR BABY'S BAPTISM

Let us turn once again to the Joyful Mysteries of the Rosary which during the past months should have become so much a part of your spiritual life. The fourth mystery commemorates the presentation of the Child Jesus in the temple. Our Blessed Lady, according to the Jewish custom, brought her Infant to the place of religious worship, the temple, and symbolically offered Him back to God.

Like Mary, you too must plan to bring your child to the church, to receive the sacrament of Baptism. This day must not be delayed for trivial reasons. A fear of baby catching a cold or a slight siege of colic are surely not justifiable excuses for unduly long postponing the administration of this sacrament.

This is your first serious obligation as a parent. Remember that in your hands rests the responsibility for your child's soul! So be willing to cooperate with the Holy Spirit by arranging for Baptism at the earliest possible date.

You anxiously counted the days and looked forward to his physical birth. Anticipate with even more eagerness his spiritual birth. For just as certainly as a feeling of happiness and accomplishment filled your heart on the day your child was born, so too will an even deeper sense of satisfaction and abiding joy be yours the day he receives the gift of eternal life in the sacrament of Baptism.

Since this is such an important event in the life of your baby, it is only right that you should make some serious and thoughtful plans for this day—the day of his birth into God's own family. Let's call this phase of your preparations for baby's coming, "preparing a spiritual layette."

The first item which you will wish to include is a Baptismal Robe. By this we are not referring to the beautiful

17

baptismal dresses that are handed down in many families. This is a lovely custom, and if such an heirloom is available in your family, you will, no doubt, be proud to use it. But when we use the term, Baptismal Robe, we mean, rather, the square of white linen used by the priest in the administration of the sacrament.

In the early days of the Church, the sacrament of Baptism was usually given by immersion. As the newly baptized stepped from the font he was presented with a white baptismal robe, symbolic of his newly granted innocence. Today, as the priest concludes the administration of the sacrament, he places on the head of the newly baptized a white linen square (which is permitted as a substitute for the robes used by the early Christians) and says:

> *"Receive this white garment,*
> *And wear it unstained*
> *To the judgment seat of our Lord Jesus Christ,*
> *That you may have everlasting life."*

Many mothers wish to provide the priest with their child's own white robe so that it may be kept as a lifetime reminder of this memorable spiritual occasion. On the anniversaries of Baptism and on First Communion day it can be used as a valuable object lesson to teach the dignity and duties of a child of God.

To avoid misunderstanding, it is well to point out that there is no one pattern for making the Baptismal Robe. The only requisite is that it be white. Some are made in the shape of loose fitting robes, and others are merely linen squares with the symbols of the seven sacraments embroidered on them. If the date of the baptism is added, a very complete spiritual record of the child's growth in Christ may be kept.

The family may also wish to provide the Baptismal Candle which is used during the ceremony and is presented to the baptized (or to the sponsor) as the priest says:

*"Receive this burning candle
And safeguard your baptism above reproach.
Keep God's commandments,
So that when the Lord comes to the marriage feast
You may meet Him in the halls of heaven
With all His Saints,
And live with Him forever and ever."*

The only requirement for the candle is that it should be of bees' wax. For practical reasons, it is well to select a heavy one that can be lighted many times, since you will wish to burn it on baptismal anniversaries and on other occasions of spiritual significance in the life of your child. You might also try your hand with brush and oil paints to draw a red Chi Rho or some other suitable symbol on the candle, to make it look more festive and "special."

There are available today many birth and baptismal announcements of a truly Catholic character. These, too, should form a part of the spiritual layette, as should some of the excellent pamphlets on Baptism which explain the full meaning of the sacrament and of the many beautiful ceremonies surrounding its administration.' It is a very good idea, too, to secure copies of the Rite of Infant Baptism to present to all who plan to attend the ceremony.

Of course, it is expected that the mother herself should make every effort to be present. And a most fitting preparation for you and your husband would be to read together the text of the baptismal rite as well as those parts of the Holy Saturday liturgy that tell of the blessing of the Baptismal font, and the blessing of the paschal Candle. It will help you to realize more deeply your dignity as Christian parents.

In some parishes the Blessing for a Mother After Childbirth is given following Baptism. Ask your pastor if this is the custom in your parish. This is a beautiful means of offering thanks to God for the safe delivery of your child and should be sought by all Catholic mothers. *The complete text of the Blessing for a Mother After Childbirth may be found on Page 11 .*

19

Give serious care and thought to the selection of the man and woman who will serve as sponsors for your child. The first requisite is that they both be practical Catholics — people who in their own lives have shown a deep appreciation for their religion: for sponsors represent Mother Church herself. Remember that in the name of your child they must make a profession of faith, and that they must assume the responsibility for his education as a Catholic in the event that you are unable to do so.

Another important matter is that of selecting a name for the baby. By all means choose a saint's name. Do not succumb to the rather common trend of naming a child for a current TV star, the girl at the corner beauty shop, or no one in particular. Give your child the name of a saint at Baptism, someone he may point to with pride, imitate in his daily life, and pray to later as his special intercessor in heaven.

Learn about your child's saint at once, so that you may begin telling him about his patron as soon as he is old enough to enjoy stories. Many Catholic families follow the beautiful custom of naming the first daughter Mary and the first son Joseph.

A powerful truth for all parents to meditate on is that when your child receives this sacrament, he becomes a son of God, an heir of heaven, a very real and vital member of the Mystical Body of Christ. He is no longer your child to do with as you wish, but a very sacred trust from Almighty God. Just as Mary accepted as her lot in life the prophetic words of Simeon on the day the Child Jesus was presented in the temple, so too, you as parents, must willingly accept from Almighty God all the sacrifices, sorrows, and work that will be required of you as parents.

Our present Holy Father, Pope Pius XII, warns of the responsibilities of parenthood bestowed by the sacrament of Baptism in the following words:

> "The souls of children given to their parents by God
> and consecrated in Baptism with the royal character
> of Christ are a sacred charge over which watches the
> jealous love of God. The same Christ who
> pronounced the words, "Suffer the little children to

come to me," for all His mercy and goodness has nevertheless threatened with fearful evils all who give scandal to those so dear to His Heart."

Fifth Mystery
Finding Jesus in the Temple
WHAT WILL YOUR CHILD BE LIKE AT TWELVE YEARS?

Let us imagine that you have in your living room a very badly worn chair which you are financially unable to replace, although it is an eye-sore to you and a continual source of embarrassment. But let us suppose, for the sake of a story, that one morning the mailman brings you a present from your mother —ten yards of beautiful hand-blocked linen. (She had probably noticed the chair on her last visit, but tactfully said nothing.) Although you are quite an amateur at sewing, you realize that her gift will make an attractive slip-cover for your problem chair.

Your first impulse certainly isn't to rush for your scissors and start cutting. As a mature individual you sit back and visualize how you wish the chair to look when your project is completed—in other words you work out a plan. Perhaps you go to the library and borrow a book containing descriptions of how to make slip-covers, possibly you consult an expert, or you may try to purchase a pattern or at least make one by carefully pinning paper or the material itself meticulously to the chair.

There is nothing haphazard about your methods. You try by all the means at your command to do a good job. You do not assume a knowledge you do not possess. You do all in your power to protect the value of the material you are working with—possibly thirty or forty dollars—so that it may serve the purpose for which it was intended.

But pause now for a moment and think—have you made any plans for the early training of the child you will soon hold in your arms? God is entrusting into your hands a human soul, whom He loves with an infinite love. You and your husband are

23

His "agents" in guarding and guiding it during its first all-important formative period.

Before you become lost in the rigidity of baby's schedule—feedings every four hours, baths, formula, and laundry—to name just a few of the things that will make a mere mention of a forty-hour week look like child's play—why not take the time to draw up a blue print of some of the things you hope to achieve during your baby's infancy and childhood?

A thoughtful consideration of these things will not only give you a goal to strive for, but a deeper understanding of life that will see you through the trying first months of baby's existence. For those first months are trying to the inexperienced mother. It is foolish to deny the fact. It is a tremendous jump, from the freedom which the average young American working girl, career woman, or student enjoys, to the restrictions motherhood as a profession requires. The lovable darling in the pink or blue bassinette makes you a virtual prisoner. An infant demands your almost constant attention.

Unless under unusual circumstances, you will consider it your own personal privilege, as well as your duty, to devote yourself to the unfolding of your child. Since Mary is our model, let us remember that she took care of her Child. It is unthinkable that she would have left Him to the care of strangers.

Some women today find frustration and drudgery in their role as mothers instead of peace and contentment. Perhaps this is due, in large part, to the fact that they look on their career of motherhood as more or less incidental. They feel it is their function according to nature, and forget it is their privilege in the order of grace. They fail to see that in bringing a child to its full perfection of body and spirit they are cooperating in a unique way with the Holy Spirit.

Since you are now on the very threshold of motherhood, it would be wise to give some serious thought to „Motherhood as a Profession.'

Perhaps in years past when our entire civilization followed a Christian pattern, when a large family was the rule, not the exception, when the home was the chief center of everyone's life, such a study was not so much neglected. Through

the natural course of events, girls acquired this knowledge since they did not frequently seek employment away from home at an early age. Today, however, nearly everyone will agree that we need to re-evaluate the role of the Catholic mother in the home.

The reader may be among those who have had the advantage of a course in Christian Marriage and Parenthood, or participation in Cana groups; but for those who have not, these days of comparative quiet before the baby comes will give an opportunity to do some helpful reading on the subject.

Perhaps our Holy Father's four point program for sanctifying family life might profitably serve as a starting point for your own study.

Our Holy Father understands the full importance of teaching by example. Thus the first point he suggests is to build a common prayer life—in other words pray with your children. This habit of prayer is the most important habit which you as a parent have the privilege and obligation of teaching your children. Long before they are actually able to participate, let them be with you as you say the family rosary. What sweeter lullaby could you possibly find—as the baby takes the final feeding of the day —than the beautiful words of the Hail Mary?

Certainly our Blessed Mother will smile with pleasure on a family praying together. It will remind her of another home long ago in Nazareth and the Child she nursed to Manhood.

Meal prayers should also be said together and with reverence. The family's consecration to the Sacred Heart ought to be renewed each First Friday. Family prayers to patron saints should all be a part of the prayer life in your home. By having the family, as a unit, take part in such simple ceremonies as the blessing and lighting of the Advent Wreath, pre-paring and blessing of the Christmas Crib, and the crowning of the Blessed Virgin Mary, deep and lasting impressions are made on the minds and hearts of your children.

Our Holy Father, Pope Pius XII, has repeatedly pointed out to parents that they must make religion a more integral part of their family life, that the future safety of the Church depends upon parents assuming this God-given-responsibility.

25

That is why it is so important for parents to realize that the child's fundamental training in religion must begin during the pre-school years. In fact, one authority has gone so far as to state that the sisters and priests in school and church can only water the seeds that the parents have implanted deeply in the character of the child during this most critical period.

The second point is to develop a common work life. Teach your children from their earliest years to help about the home. Let them learn from the time they are toddlers that the home is really a co-operative enterprise—that everyone must do his share. An extra pair of hands at the kitchen sink as you wash the dishes—ten sticky fingers at the mixing bowl—of course they're a nuisance! But if you shoo the children off to play whenever they plead with you for a chance to help, how do you expect them, as they grow more capable, to do these chores without constant prodding on your part, and constant grumbling on theirs?

Give them the opportunity to learn the sense of joy and satisfaction that comes from a job well done. Household chores will not only keep them closer to the home, but will develop within them a sense of responsibility necessary to their growing into adult-hood.

Another point. Psychologists frequently warn parents not to take every element of struggle out of their children's lives— for growth, to a large extent is dependent upon struggle. In other words, let your children work for some of the things they want. If you wish them to mature into self-reliant adults, give them the opportunity to do some constructive work during childhood and adolescence. By your example as parents, rather than by words, impress upon your children a deep respect for the dignity of work.

The third step in building a sanctified family is a common social life. Let your family as a unit plan activities—family feast day parties, fishing trips, picnics. Utilize to the fullest the opportunities you have for companionship with your children. Don't let them develop the attitude that to have fun they must "get away" from Mother and Dad.

Direct their recreation into creative crafts, constructive hobbies, music, group reading. It is a serious mistake to allow children to limit all their recreation to such passive entertainment as television, radio, or the movies. Undoubtedly, it will require effort and planning on your part to develop a well-rounded social life for your family as a unit, but a happy contented family will pay dividends in the years to come.

This leads naturally to the fourth point—the development within your children of a deep sense of family loyalty—an espirit de corps. Psychologists tell us that one of the fundamental needs of a child is to feel that he really belongs to a group, and to know that he contributes something unique to the group as a whole. Children, therefore, should be taught to think of the common good of the family, to be devoted to their brothers and sisters and to stand by them in time of need—to share with them their joys.

Even the faithful performance of chores should be viewed in this light of family loyalty. All this will not only make them better members of their school and community group, but more patriotic citizens, and above all else, loyal and faithful members of the Mystical Body of Christ.

Through these four points suggested by our Holy Father, you should be able to teach your children to lead lives of purpose — impressing upon them frequently the difference between success in the form of such tangibles as money, white-walled convertibles, closets full of clothes, and success as God sees it: a heart filled with sanctifying grace.

If you resolve now, at the very outset of your career as a mother, to build your family life on such a set of principles as these suggested by our Holy Father—keeping constantly before you the humble home of the Holy Family as your guide and inspiration—rest assured that with Mary's help you will bring your child to his Confirmation Day, worthy to become a stalwart soldier in the army of Jesus Christ.

TRADITIONAL
BLESSINGS
FOR
MOTHERS

******

BLESSING
OF AN EXPECTANT MOTHER

V. Our help is in the name of the Lord.
R. Who made heaven and earth.
V. Save Thy servant, Lord.
R. For she puts her hope, O God, in Thee.
V. Be a tower of strength for her, O Lord.
R. Against Enemy attack.
V. Let not the Enemy have power against her.
R. Nor the son of evil come near to harm her.
V. O Lord, send her aid from Thy holy place.
R. And guard her from Sion.
V. O Lord, hear my prayer.
R. And let my cry come unto Thee.
V. The Lord be with thee.
R. And with thy spirit.

Let us pray.
Almighty, everlasting God, Thou hast granted Thy servants in the profession of the true Faith, to show forth the glory of the eternal Trinity and to adore Its Unity in the power of Its majesty. We ask that Thy servant, N., by her constancy in that Faith, may ever be safeguarded against all adversity. Through Christ our Lord.
R. *Amen.*

Let us pray.
O Lord God, Creator of all, Thou art mighty and awe-inspiring, just and merciful; Thou alone art kind and loving and didst set Israel free from every evil, making our fathers Thy chosen people. Thou didst sanctify them by the power of Thy Spirit and by the co-working of the Holy Ghost, didst prepare the

body and soul of the glorious Virgin Mary to become a worthy home for Thy Son. Thou didst fill John the Baptist with the Holy Ghost, making him leap with joy in his mother's womb. Accept now the offering of the contrite heart and the ardent desire of Thy servant, N., who humbly petitions Thee for the welfare of the child which Thou didst grant her to conceive. Protect the work which is Thine and guard it from all the deceit and harm of our bitter Enemy. May the hand of Thy mercy assist her delivery, and may her child see the light of day without harm; may it be kept safe for the holy rebirth of Baptism, serve Thee always in all things, and thereby merit everlasting life. Through the same Christ our Lord.

R. Amen.

The priest then sprinkles the woman with holy water, and prays.

Psalm 66

May God have pity on us and bless us; *
may He let His face shine upon us.
So may your way be known upon the earth; *
among all nations, your salvation.
May the peoples praise you; O God; *
may all the peoples praise you!
May the nations be glad and exult
because you rule the peoples in equity; *
the nations on the earth you guide.
May the peoples praise you, O God; *
may all the peoples praise you.
The earth has yielded its fruits; *
God, our God, has blessed us.
May God bless us, *
and may all the ends of the earth fear Him!
Glory be to the Father, and to the Son, *
and to the Holy Ghost.
As it was in the beginning, is now, and ever shall be
world without end. Amen.

32

V. Let us praise the Father and the Son with the Holy Ghost.
R. Let us praise and glorify Him forever.
V. To His angels God has given charge over you.
R. To guard you in all your ways.
V. O Lord, hear my prayer.
R. And let my cry come unto Thee.
V. The Lord be with thee.
R. And with thy spirit.

Let us pray.
Visit this dwelling we beg Thee, O Lord, and drive far from it and from this Thy servant, **N.**, all the snares of the Enemy. May Thy holy angels dwell here to preserve her and her child in peace, and may Thy blessing be ever upon her. Save them, O almighty God, and bestow upon them Thy unfailing light. Through Christ our Lord.
R. *Amen.*
May the blessing of Almighty God, the Father, the Son, and Holy Spirit, come down upon you and your child, and remain forever.
Amen.

****

BLESSING
OF A MOTHER AFTER CHILDBIRTH

Vested in surplice and white stole, the priest with his server proceeds to the entrance of the church where the mother with her baptized child awaits him holding a lighted candle. He sprinkles them and all the others present with holy water, saying:

V. Our help is in the name of the Lord.
R. Who made heaven and earth.

Ant. She shall receive the Lord's blessing, and mercy from God, her Savior, because she is of the generation who seek the Lord

Psalm 23

The Lord's are the earth and its fullness; *
the world and those who dwell in it.
For He founded it upon the seas *
and established it upon the rivers.
Who can ascend the mountain of the Lord?
or who may stand in His holy place?
He whose hands are sinless, whose heart is clean,
who desires not what is vain,
nor swears deceitfully to his neighbor.
He shall receive a blessing from the Lord, *
a reward from God his savior.
Such is the race that seeks for him, *
that seeks the face of the God of Jacob.
Lift up, O gates, your lintels; *
reach up, you ancient portals,
that the king of glory may come in!
Who is this king of glory? *
The Lord, strong and mighty,
the Lord, mighty in battle.
Lift up, O gates, your lintels; *
reach up, you ancient portals,

35

that the king of glory may come in!
Who is this king of glory? *
The Lord of hosts; he is the king of glory.
Glory be to the Father, and to the Son, *
and to the Holy Ghost.
As it was in the beginning, is now, and ever shall be,
world without end. Amen.

Ant. She shall receive the Lord's blessing, and mercy from God, her Savior, because she is of the generation who seek the Lord.

The priest puts the end of the stole in the woman's hand and leads her toward the altar, saying:

> Enter God's temple. Adore the Son of the blessed Virgin Mary who has given you fruitfulness of offspring.

The mother kneels on the altar step and is grateful to God.
V. Lord, have mercy.
R. Christ, have mercy. Lord, have mercy. ,
V. Our Father (silently).
And lead us not into temptation.
R. But deliver us from evil.
V. Save Thy servant, Lord.
R. For she puts her hope, O God, in Thee.
V. O Lord, send her aid from Thy holy place.
R. And guard over her from Sion.
V. Let not the Enemy have power against her.
R. Nor the son of evil come near to harm her.
V. O Lord, hear my prayer.
R. And let my cry come unto Thee.
V. The Lord be with thee.
R. And with thy spirit.

> *Let us pray.*
> Almighty, everlasting God, by the child-bearing of Blessed Virgin Mary Thou hast turned the pains of child-bearing into joy for Thy faithful. Look now

with kindness on this Thy servant, who comes rejoicing to Thy holy temple to render thanks to Thee, and grant that after this life she and her child may, by the merits and intercession of the Blessed Virgin Mary, gain the joys of everlasting happiness. Through Christ our Lord.
R. *Amen.*

The priest sprinkles mother and child with holy water, saying:
May the peace and blessing of almighty God, the Father, the Son, and Holy Spirit, come down upon thee, and remain forever.
R. *Amen.*

39